# Luke Hereford

Luke is a queer theatre maker, based in Cardiff, who trained at Royal Welsh College of Music and Drama. As Director and Assistant/Associate Director, projects include *Queerway* (Leeway Productions / WMC), *Vincent River* (Welsh Premiere, No Boundaries), *Where Do Little Birds Go?* (Cardiff Fringe Theatre Festival), *The Last Five Years* (Leeway Productions), *The Motherf\*\*\*er with the Hat* (Tron, Glasgow / Sherman Theatre, Cardiff), *The Wind in the Willows* (Sherman Theatre, Cardiff) and *Blackbird* (The Other Room).

As visiting Director for University of Wales Trinity St. David/ WAVDA, he has Directed *Xanadu, A New Brain, Spring Awakening, Growth,* and a new Stephen Sondheim revue *Every Day a Little Death* co-conceived with David George Harrington. In 2018, Luke was a part of The Carne Trust/JMK Directors programme for Sherman Theatre, and in 2019 he was the Welsh representative for Lincoln Center Theater Directors Lab in New York.

Luke is also an accomplished drag artist, Esther Parade, winning *Drag at the Stag* in 2021, the inaugural drag competition at Above the Stag Theatre, and was a national semi-finalist for *Drag Idol UK* in 2022. Esther runs a monthly Drag cabaret night in Cardiff, *CHAOS.*

First published in the UK in 2023 by Aurora Metro Publications Ltd
80 Hill Rise, Richmond, TW10 6UB
www.aurorametro.com    info@aurorametro.com
twitter @aurorametro FB/AuroraMetroBooks

Production: Yasmeen Doogue-Khan
For rights enquiries including performing rights, contact the publisher:
info@aurorametro.com

Printed on sustainably resourced paper.
ISBN: 978-1-912430-89-5
ISBN: 978-1-912430-90-1

# GRANDMOTHER'S CLOSET

## LUKE HEREFORD

AURORA METRO BOOKS

*This play is for anyone who has ever enjoyed dressing up. For anyone who's ever wished they could be their favourite Diva, even just for a fleeting moment.*

*For my best Judys, Michael Lowe and Meg Fitzpatrick.*

*But most of all this play is for my grandmother, Joan.*

– Luke Hereford

# CONTENTS

# WALES MILLENNIUM CENTRE

Wales Millennium Centre is a home for the arts in Wales, a cauldron of creativity for the nation. They fire imaginations by creating their own theatre productions, festivals and digital experiences – as well as curating world-class, critically acclaimed touring productions – from musical theatre and comedy to dance and cabaret. They kindle emerging talents with their own fresh, provocative and popular productions, rooted in Welsh culture. They're also a charity, collaborating with organisations, communities and young people to make the arts accessible to everyone. They ignite a passion for the arts with life-changing learning experiences and chances to shine in the spotlight.

*Grandmother's Closet* was first performed 20th April 2022, at the Weston Studio, Wales Millennium Centre, Cardiff, under the title *Grandmother's Closet (and what I found there...)*

## Cast

| | |
|---|---|
| Writer/Performer | Luke Hereford (he/they) |
| Pianist/Musical Director | David George Harrington (he/him) |

## Creative Team

| | |
|---|---|
| Director | François Pandolfo (he/him) |
| Production Designer | Carl Davies (he/him) |
| Lighting Designer | Jane Lalljee (she/her) |
| Sound Designer | Josh Bowles (he/him) |
| Associate Director | Nerida Bradley (she/they) |
| Movement Director | Jo Fong (she/her) |
| Arrangements | David George Harrington (he/him) and Josh Bowles (he/him) |
| Poster design | Toby Nelmes (he/him) and Kirsten McTernan (she/her) |

## Production Team

| | |
|---|---|
| Stage Manager | Philippa Mannion (she/her) |
| Technical Manager | Martin Hunt (he/him) |
| Caption Operator | Daf Weeks (he/him) |
| Dementia Advisor | Ceri Ann Harris (she/her) |
| Access Coordinators | Steph Back (she/her) Garrin Clarke (he/him) |
| Producer | Peter Darney (he/him) |

*Grandmother's Closet* ran at Cairns Lecture Hall, Summerhall for Edinburgh Fringe Festival 3rd – 28th August 2022 with the following changes and additions to the company:

## Cast

Pianist                           Bobby Harding (they/them)

## Creative Team

Dramaturg                     Sarah Page (she/her)

## Production Team

Technicians                  Euan Jackson (he/him)
                              Chris Kutya (he/him)
                              Allie Pates (they/them)

*Special thanks to:*

Corner Shop PR, Caerwent Body Repairs, Esmée Fairbairn Foundation, Auntie Margaret Media, LGBTQYMRU, The Queer Emporium, South Wales Life, Buzz Magazine, Bristol Pride, National Theatre Wales, Taking Flight Theatre, Summerhall, The Wardrobe Theatre, The Courtyard Theatre, Det Andre Teatret Oslo, Silvia Rodriguez Gimenez, Daryn Carter, Chris Lloyd, Kirsten McTernan, Ric Watts, Seiriol Davies, Phil Jones, Rebecca Jade Hammond, Beth Granville, Katie Elin-Salt, Angharad Lee, Le Gateaux Chocolat, Twm Bollen-Molloy, Ben Tyreman, Oliver Williams and Guto Rhun.

Cyngor Celfyddydau Cymru
Arts Council of Wales

# BIOGRAPHIES

## Bobby Harding (they/them) – Pianist

Bobby is a wearer of many hats. Born in Walsall, they are not only a freelance theatre producer with a passion for supporting radical queer work and platforming fellow working-class artists, but they are also a very experienced musical director and accompanist, having worked in London for many years after training at Trinity Laban Conservatoire of Music and Dance. They joined the *Grandmother's Closet* team as the magical mirror maestro in 2022 to play for the Edinburgh Fringe run and have loved every bonkers minute since. Their advice for future pianists of the show would be to watch every music video for each song at least ten times, channel all the camp you can muster... and be utterly fabulous.

## François Pandolfo (he/him) – Director

François trained at East 15 Acting School. His most notable television credits include: *Doctor Who*, *Tati's Hotel*, *Casualty*, *Doctors*, *Baker Boys*, *The Tuckers*, *Eastenders*, *Wasted*, *Big Boys*. His radio work includes: *The House That Eileen Built*, *My Own Private Gondolier*, *The Tinner's Corpse*, *Becoming Betty*, *Tracks*, *Stalingrad*, *Torchwood*, *Foiled*, *The Miser*, *Broken Colours*. François' theatre credits include: *Right Where We Left Us* (Chippy Lane Productions); for Sherman Theatre: *The Taming of the Shrew*, *The Motherf\*\*\*er with the Hat*, *Alice in Wonderland*; for Theatr Clwyd: *A Small Family Business*, *Macbeth*, *A History of Falling Things;* for National Theatre Wales: *Lifted by Beauty*, *Mission Control*; for Mappa Mundi: *The Compleat Female Stage*

*Beauty*, *A Midsummer Night's Dream*, *Wuthering Heights* (Aberystwyth Arts Centre), *The Magic Flute* (Welsh National Opera), *Double Vision* (GaggleBabble), *Bad Girls* (Polka Theatre). François is the co-director of his own Cardiff-born theatre company: difficult|stage. Productions include: *A Cold Spread*, *The World of Work*, *Alix in Wundergarten*, *Looking Through Glass* and award-winning show *An Audience with Milly-Liu*. *Grandmother's Closet* is Francois' directorial debut.

## David George Harrington (he/him) – Musical Director/Arrangements

David is a composer, arranger and musical director who has worked and performed professionally for twelve years all over the UK. His commercial clients include Kylie Minogue, Justin Bieber, Katherine Jenkins, Connie Fisher, Jonny Wilkes, Aled Jones, Shirley Bassey, and he has had music performed by the London Philharmonic and London Concert Orchestras, Welsh National Opera, BBC National Orchestra of Wales, Cory Brass Band and soloists from the London Symphony Orchestra. He regularly arranges /orchestrates for Decca Records, Warner Music Group, and has had music broadcast on ITV, BBC, and BBC Radio 2. Recently David has produced music for the Platinum Jubilee celebrations and has toured with viral vocal group *Welsh of The West End*. David frequently collaborates with leading West End performers, plays for cabarets, revues corporate gigs at home and abroad, lectures at the Royal Welsh College of Music and Drama, and is currently writing and workshopping two new musicals.

## Carl Davies (he/him) – Designer

Carl trained at the Royal Welsh College of Music and Drama, graduating in 2004. Credits include, theatre: *Operation Julie*, *The Eye of the Storm* (Theatr Na Nog); *There is a War* (Italia Conti); *Pijin* (Theatr Iolo /Theatr Genedlaethol); *Gwlad Yr Asyn*, *Nansi*, *Blodeuwedd* (Theatr Genedlaethol); *Cotton Fingers*, *Peggy's Song*, *The Stick Maker Tales, For All I Care*, *Come Back Tomorrow* (National Theatre Wales); Hoof (Theatr Iolo); *Where all Paths Lead*, *Last Orders*, *Box of Delights* (2faced Dance Company); *Dead Good*, *A Brave Face*, *The Best Thing*, *Sharing Joy*, *Finding Joy*, *Nursing Lives* (Vamos Theatre); *Marry Me A Little*, *Hopeless Romantics*, *Great Expectations*, *The Goal*, *Lord of the Flies* (Courtyard Theatre Hereford); *All But Gone*, *The Effect*, *A Number*, *Looking Through Glass* (The Other Room); *The Eye of the Storm*, (Theatr Na Nog); *The Dreaming* (Lichfield Garrick); *The Trials of Oscar Wilde*, *Still Life*, *Stage Beauty*, *Much Ado About Nothing*, *Dangerous Liaisons*, (Mappa Mundi); *Belonging* (Re-Live); *Oliver Twist*, *Oh No Not Snow*, *Immune*, *Honk*, *Sweeney Todd* (Royal & Derngate); *Hansel and Gretel*, *The Mikado*, *Madam Butterfly* (Co Opera Co); film: *Cold* (Open Sky); *Hush Now*, *Last Call* (Feral Productions).

## Jane Lalljee (she/her) – Lighting Designer

Jane is a lighting designer based in Cardiff. Upcoming projects: *Songs From Far Away* starring Will Young (HOME, Manchester), *Welsh Radical, The Cost of Living* (National Theatre Wales). Recent projects include: *Aladdin* (Harrogate Theatre), *Constellations* (Stephen Joseph Theatre), *Right Where We Left Us* (Chippy Lane Productions), *Rose* starring Maureen Lipman (Hope

Mill, Manchester, Park Theatre, London), *One Man, Two Guvnors* (Bolton Octagon/Theatre by the Lake/ Liverpool Everyman and Playhouse), *Circle of Fifths* (National Theatre Wales), *I Wanna Be Yours* (Leeds Playhouse), *Grandmother's Closet* (Wales Millennium Centre), *The House With Chicken Legs* (Les Enfants Terribles/HOME), *Wind in the Willows* (Taunton Brewhouse), *Peter Pan* (Bolton Octagon), *Antigone* (Storyhouse), *Meet Me at Dawn* (HER Productions/Hope Mill), *Ghost Light* (Concept and lead artist at Ffwrnes Theatr), *The Storm* (M6 Theatre), *Dr Korczak's Example* (Leeds Playhouse), *Giraffes Can't Dance* (Leicester Curve), *Feathers* (National Dance Company of Wales), *Cotton Fingers* (National Theatre Wales), *Peeling* (Taking Flight), *The Last Five Years* (Leeway Productions).

## Josh Bowles (he/him) – Sound Designer/ Arrangements

Josh is a Cardiff-based sound designer / engineer and composer. Primarily working in theatre, he has designed and/or engineered on *The Boy With Two Hearts* (National Theatre / Wales Millenium Centre), *Queerway* (Leeway Productions / Wales Millenium Centre), *A New Brain* (University of Wales Trinity Saint David), *Dance To The Bone* (Sherman Theatre), *XXXmas Carol* (Big Loop Theatre / Wales Millenium Centre), *Crafangau / Claws* (Sherman Theatre), *Lovecraft* [Not The Sex Shop In Cardiff] (Carys Eleri / Wales Millenium Centre), *Crave* (The Other Room / Royal Welsh College of Music & Drama), *Cardiff Boy* (Red Oak Theatre / The Other Room), *Vincent River* (No Boundaries Theatre), *Dames* (Siberian Lights), *Alice In Wonderland* (Sherman Theatre), *Llais/Voice* (Cwmni Pluen / Sherman Theatre). Josh also works as a live sound recordist and mixer, with recent projects including *Codi*, and *Wild Thoughts* (National Dance Company Wales), *10 Minute Musicals* (Leeway Productions) and various projects for Horizons / Gorwelion (BBC Radio Wales).

## Jo Fong (she/her) – Movement Director

Jo Fong is a creative associate with the Wales Millennium Centre. She has been dancing and making for thirty years and began her career with Rosas, Rambert and DV8 Physical Theatre. She lives in Wales and her creative work reflects the need in these times for people to come together. Her artistic practice is an evolving, collaborative approach which puts ideas around belonging or forming community in the forefront. Recent performances and events: *Ways of Being Together*, *Neither Here Nor There*, *To Tell You the Truth*, *Our Land*, *What Will People Need?*, *Nettles: How to Disagree?*, *The Sun's Come Out* created in collaboration with artist Sonia Hughes, *A Brief History of Difference* with Das Clarks, and *Marathon of Intimacies* with artist Anushiye Yarnell. Jo is touring with a performance called *The Rest of Our Lives* created with clown and circus maker George Orange.

## Nerida Bradley (she/they) – Associate Director

Nerida is a queer theatre director, writer and facilitator. She is a creative associate at the Wales Millennium Centre and former trainee director at The Other Room. Director credits: *CHOO CHOO! You Are Not Your Thoughts* (Stammermouth Theatre), *Revolt. She Said. Revolt Again.* (The Other Room), *The Love Thief* (Sherman Theatre). Assistant director credits: *The Lion, The B!tch and the*

*Wardrobe* (Wales Millennium Centre), *Constellation Street* (National Theatre Wales/The Other Room), *Microwave* (Run Amok Theatre Company), *Crave* (The Other Room), *Cardiff Boy* (Red Oak Theatre Company), *All But Gone* (The Other Room), *hang* (Run Amok Theatre Company).

## Philippa Mannion (she/her) – Stage Manager

Philippa is a Cardiff-based stage manager, who also writes and produces. Her stage manager credits include: *User Not Found* (Dante or Die – UK and International Tour), *Take On Me* (Dante or Die – UK Tour), *Malory Towers* (Wise Children), *Tiddly Prom* (Arts Active), *Jade City* (Vault Festival / Bunker Theatre), *Nightmare Scenario* (Operasonic), *XXXmas Carol* (Wales Millennium Centre), *Revolt. She Said. Revolt Again* (The Other Room), *An Audience with Milly-Liu* (Difficult Stage in assoc. with Sherman Theatre / Edinburgh Festival Fringe), and *The Lion, The B!tch and The Wardrobe* (Wales Millennium Centre). Philippa is also a production supervisor at Royal Welsh College of Music and Drama.

## Sarah Page (she/her) – Dramaturg

Sarah took part in Soho Theatre's *Young Writers'* programme and the Royal Court Theatre's *Young Writers'* and *Studio* groups. The winner of two *Peggy Ramsay Awards* and a finalist for the *Nick Darke Writer's Award*, Sarah's plays include *Punts* (Kuleshov Theatre/ Theatre503, published by Bloomsbury), *The Sweethearts* (Finborough Theatre, published by Oberon Books and Samuel French), *The Night My Parents Went Away*

(Milano Theatre Festival) and *Pilgrims* (Raise Dark/ Etcetera Theatre). Her new play, *Mrs. Wickham*, for Audible Originals, has just been recorded with a cast including Jessie Buckley and Johnny Flynn. Sarah was one of the writers on the BBC's *New Talent Hotlist* and is an alumnus of the *4Screenwriting* programme and BBC's *Drama Writers' programme 2019*. She has several original TV shows and two feature films in development. As well as being a writer, Sarah is an experienced script editor/reader, mentor, dramaturg and workshop leader with a passion for encouraging underrepresented voices in theatre, film and TV. She is represented by Ikenna Obiekwe at Independent Talent.

## Peter Darney (he/him) – Producer

Peter trained at Royal Welsh College of Music and Drama and  is a producer, writer and director. He is a resident producer at Wales Millennium Centre and an associate artist at the King's Head Theatre. Producing credits include: *Grandmother's Closet* (Wales Millennium Centre/Summerhall), *XXXmas Carol* (Wales Millennium Centre), and *Free and Proud* (Theatre 503/Assembly Festival). Producer and director credits include: *The Revengers Tragedy* (The Rose Playhouse), *James Dean Is Dead* (Jermyn Street Theatre), and *Mysterious Skin* (Gilded Balloon, The Drill Hall, Teacher's Club, Dublin). As a writer director, Peter's play *5 Guys Chillin'* was named one of *"Ten Plays That Shaped Queer Theatre History"* by the *Evening Standard* and has played extensively in London, Edinburgh, Off-Broadway, Dublin, Sydney, Toronto and Paris.

David George Harrington and Luke Hereford. Photo: Chris Lloyd

Above and below: Luke Hereford, photos Kirsten McTernan

Above and below: Luke Hereford, photos Kirsten McTernan

# PREFACE

As I write this and imagine opening my nonna's ceiling-to-floor, Italian, walnut-wood wardrobe, I can instantly smell her fragrance lingering within – Chanel No. 5 – and it transports me back to a time when my imagination was at its most influential – where my unpolluted, young senses absorbed delights so honestly.

The mixture of materials and vibrant colours being so carefully preserved inside was a doorway into what it meant to feel glamorous, watched, and considered. The setting, my nonna's bedroom, with its pristine three-mirror dressing-table, humongous Elnett hairspray cans and thick, cream shagpile represented a place of safety, dress-up and ritual. *Grandmother's Closet* celebrates these sacred settings, wherever they may be, and reminds us of the importance of our relationships with these spaces and the people that inhabit them.

To be invited into these magical yet mundane worlds, to discover a sense of self by exploring the abundant troves they hold is one of life's privileges. The people who are willing to share them with us, equally need to be treasured and remembered, for they are the gatekeepers who helped shape us.

*Grandmother's Closet* pays homage to one of these selfless icons, Joan Doreen Hereford, and the special bond with her grandson, Luke. Through the power of her closet and her steadfast, no-nonsense, dignified attitude towards life, Joan created an oasis for Luke to explore his own identity and face an often scary world. With her memory quickly fading, will Luke eventually be ready to face the world alone?

As I close my own nonna's wardrobe... I fear we never are ready, but we can certainly try to face the world without them.

To all the Nans, Nonnas, Aunties, Mam-gus, Mams, Nains, Step-Mums and guardians alike, thank you for protecting, encouraging and inspiring. You know who you are. You helped us dance to our own rhythm.

– Director, François Pandolfo

François Pandolfo. Photo: Chris Lloyd

# GRANDMOTHER'S CLOSET

by

## Luke Hereford

## CHARACTERS

**LUKE**
**THE PIANIST**

*This play was intended to be performed as a monologue by one actor with musical accompaniment but it could be performed by a group of actors. Other characters which feature in the play include:*

**NAN**
**UNCLE**
**DAD**
**MOTHER**
**WOMAN AT PRIDE**
**JAC**
**SINGER (JAKE SHEARS)**
**KYLIE MINOGUE**
**KATE BUSH**
**JUDY GARLAND**

*Setting:*

We are in a remembered version of Luke's grandmother's old house – *Waun Fawr*. Fragmented, disjointed, details missing. As if he's pieced it together from fading memories.

*Approach:*

The text is playful, and this is reflected in Luke's interaction with the audience – to whom the majority of the play is directed. It's as if they are guests at his nan's home.

This playfulness also extends to the pianist, who is a crucial part of allowing the fever dream of memories to live. Their relationship should be indulgent and ridiculous, but also steadfast and tender. The Pianist does not have any spoken lines, but should be a larger than life presence at opportune moments. Backing vocals are enthusiastically encouraged.

Much of the play is addressed directly to his grandmother (marked with bracketed text: "to Nan") wherever she may be. In the original staging, Nan was not visible within the space.

Throughout the play, Luke embodies various other characters, from his homophobic Uncle, right through to his favourite iconic Divas – Kylie Minogue, Judy Garland, Jake Shears et. al. There should be a clear distinction between the embodiment of each of these different characters.

*A wardrobe, a piano and maybe some other furniture are covered in dust sheets. A washing machine is hidden somewhere in the space.*

*He is wearing nothing but some fabulous underwear, and might be talking to audience members as they enter. Family party vibes. The playlist reflects this too, but with a suspiciously queer undertone. Music from George Michael, Prefab Sprout, Fleetwood Mac, Sylvester.*

*Eventually, the light finds him.*

**LUKE**     It's my nan's ninetieth birthday today! So we're having a big party, at her old house: *Waun Fawr*. It's the most vibrant this house has been in a long time. Very out of character for the sleepy village of Caerwent. There's a beige buffet on the go. Auntie P's famous vol-au-vents. Mum in a black sequined dress – she looks like she's in an am-dram production of *Chicago*. And all the blokes from the family in their short-sleeved plaid shirts, shiny hair gel and smart jeans... is there such a thing?

Then there's me. Eyes lined. Triple velour. Jacket, trousers, shoes. Out of place in this crowd of homeowners, teaching assistants and smart jeans.

*In the crowd, he spots his nan –*

*(to Nan)*     Until you walk in. Escorted like royalty, and everyone's attention turns to the woman of the hour. A crowd surrounds you; everyone is desperate to catch a glimpse – see what glamorous outfit you've chosen. See if your hair is still as pitch-black and perfect as legend would have it. You humbly make your way through the crowd, then, you spot me. Those famous eyes of yours – one brown and one blue – light up, and a wicked smile grows on your perfectly painted lips as you pull me in for one of your legendary *cwtches* and whisper in my ear:

*(Nan)*     "Oh, my sunshine, you look gorgeous."

Everyone says I take after my nan, in terms of... glamour. But, really I could never come close. Though we are both head to toe in black and gold tonight. Coincidence? Doubt it.

Riding high on her appreciation of my outfit, I step outside for a cigarette, followed by... let's call him Uncle Ignorant. He takes one look at me, and says:

*(Uncle)*     "Ooh, darling! Don't you look fancy?"

He makes some boring joke about makeup, and velvet jackets.

*( younger self)* "It's velour, actually!"

So I tear myself away, give him the excuse that I'm cold.

*(Uncle)*     "Go on then. You faggot."

And everything seems to stop. I can't believe that this is happening. And here. In these safe, sacred, walls. Nan's old house. I find my way inside, looking for her. Because she'll back me up, give me some confidence, some self-belief. She always has. She always will.

*(to Nan)*    But, you'd gone, Nan. I tried to find you, but you'd gone. Mum says something about you being tired, so Auntie Ann thought it was best to take you home, which is silly, because you've only been here for an hour or two. It's your birthday, your party. Your ninetieth. And I need you.

I hurry upstairs, not wanting Uncle Ignorant to see me, or the tears forming in my eyes. He knew he had to do this when Nan wasn't here.

I escape to my favourite corner of *Waun Fawr* – the little dressing nook, just outside of Nan's bedroom. And in the mirror, I see the bedroom door, wide open. I step into the room, turn on the lights, and, staring back at me, is Nan's wardrobe. Beckoning.

Just as I remember it. And with Nan gone, I need to find strength somewhere else. So without a second thought, I throw open the doors of my grandmother's closet...

*A very theatrical moment. He throws the dust sheet off the wardrobe, and steps inside. A pianist appears! Lights! Dry ice! Bubbles! Culminating in him "coming out of the closet" in a beautiful, vintage, turquoise floor-length gown that belonged to his grandmother. He sings a triumphant, defiant mashup of songs:*

*"Dress You Up" / "Material Girl" by Madonna*

I looked fucking fabulous. A fucking fabulous, faggot!

*The song ends – he soaks in the rapturous applause.*

Nobody batted an eyelid.

But, by the time I'd plucked up the courage to make my way back downstairs and face Uncle Ignorant with my newfound strength, he'd already left. Still, I stay in my 100% polyester suit of armour for the rest of the night.

*(to Nan)*    It's what you would have expected of me, Nan. So, how did I do? And what do you think of the lipstick? Is it close? Okay... I'll keep trying.

*He wipes off a shade of lipstick that he'd put on during the song. Then he takes off the dress, and ceremoniously puts it into the washing machine.*

My grandmother, Joan Doreen Hereford, née Chappel, is my original ally. My first glimpse of the power of the iconic woman. See, I wasn't born with... power, strength, a wide selection of makeshift suits of armour with which to combat everyday homophobia.

*(to Nan)*     Whenever you aren't by my side, I've had to find the parts of you that make me strong elsewhere. Any guesses where? I'll show you.

*An indulgent moment – yes, really, another one already – underscored by the "Overture" from "The Wizard of Oz". After getting caught up in the tornado for a moment, it ends abruptly. He's ready to start at the very beginning...*

*(to Nan)*     For me, Nan, it all starts with your old house. *Waun Fawr.* This angular pebbledash paradise, this 1970s' issue of *Ideal Home*, frozen in time. Do you remember the floral-patterned carpets in every room? The trinkets on every shelf, from your many travels? Most importantly, the thrill of playing dress up, in your wardrobe?

Most weekends, at five years old, I could be found in Nan's bedroom. Gazing up at imposing mirrored doors, pressing my ear against them to be seduced by the enticing whispers coming from inside. It would never be long before I would give in to their siren song, and throw open the doors, pouring through decades of dresses, power suits, and salopettes – the glamour, the drama, the polyester!

Nan's wardrobe was the ideal costume department for the many performances I would give in the living room at five years old. They were the real deal. Often inspired by whichever old Hollywood epic from Nan's VHS collection I was obsessed with that week. But there was one obsession that changed it all. Twenty-four years later, it's still going strong. You knew it was coming folks. My Judy Garland era.

*The "Munchkinland" music from "The Wizard of Oz plays"...*

I'll never forget the first time I witnessed the moment she steps from her sepia-toned life and into glorious technicolour as that incredible music plays. I mean, if that isn't a metaphor for coming out of the closet, nothing is... but there was another moment. One that I simply had to perform for an unwilling audience of close family members.

The butterflies in my five-year-old stomach flutter, as I prepare for my swansong, trawling through Nan's wardrobe, trying to find the perfect costume. But... *nothing is right*!

I'm about to give up all hope of fulfilling my destiny as a Judy Garland living room legend, when Nan sails in. And she stops my almost diva strop before I become insufferable... even more, insufferable.

And in an instant, she finds me the perfect gown. A moment of pure solidarity.

*He steps into the wardrobe...*

I can sense the magic that this dress possesses, and it's intoxicating. The faint smell of Nan's perfume lingers on the collar from when last she wore it. I'm ready. I could not fail.

A wicked smile on her perfectly painted lips says:

*(Nan)*      "Don't let me down, sunshine."

And I don't.

*He is in a gown nothing like Judy Garland's "Trolley Song" dress. But he'll make it work, as he sings:*

*"The Trolley Song" from "Meet Me In St. Louis"*

> The scattered, unenthusiastic applause is dampened by the unforgiving acoustics of Waun Fawr's artex. But it sounds to this five-year-old like the eruption of Carnegie Hall. Maybe that's because Nan's standing ovation is enough to make up for everyone else's lack of enthusiasm. I bow. Low. Humbled by my adoring fans... fan.

*He takes the dress off, and places it delicately into the washing machine.*

*(to Nan)*        That's you, Nan. You were my biggest fan. And you were always there, helping me find my way through whichever obsession was next. *Peter Pan*: you made me a costume identical to the film. Trying to fly, I suspended myself from the wall-lamp in your bedroom. *The Little Mermaid*: I flooded your upstairs bathroom because I thought the bidet would make for an excellent water fountain. It didn't.

*(to Nan)*        What about when Dad and I first discovered the two divas? On *Top of the Pops*.

Dad fancies the pants off both of them. For Dad, it's all in the slip of a thigh in a slinky jumpsuit. For me, it's the soft bevel of her leg that leads to the thigh reveal. For Dad, it's pausing the music video to make out the shape of her nether regions beneath her white organza gown. For me, it's amazement at her flawless cartwheels.

I try to want them the same way that Dad wants them, so that he might admire me the same way he admires our two divas... well, not exactly the same way... daddy issues.

But we watch them together, and they're calling me... in a different way. They're whispering, something that I know they don't whisper to Dad...

*(The divas)* "Give us a try..."

*He spots a dustsheet. No. A multi-diva embodying garment! He wraps himself in it, at first, emulating Kylie Minogue's iconic "Can't Get You Out of My Head" outfit, then he uses it to embody both Kylie and Kate Bush, as he sings a jubilant mashup of songs:*

*"WOW" by Kylie Minogue / "Wow" by Kate Bush*

*After the song ends, he falls back into reality. Realising he got very carried away with that sheet, and the song, he sheepishly puts it in the washing machine.*

Okay, I'm never going to be a Kylie backup dancer. But my dad's never going to sleep with Kate Bush either, so...

*(to Nan)* I think you always knew that I never quite liked them the same way Dad liked them. But it didn't matter to you. You just loved seeing my eyes light up as I watched them dancing on *Top of the Pops*.

Not just the two divas. We saw Boy George on *Top of the Pops* once. Dad just scoffed:

*(Dad)* "Bloody poof."

I didn't know what it meant at the time. But, I knew it wasn't a good thing. Which is a shame, 'cause I thought his makeup was fabulous! Still, after that, I knew I'd have to keep my first real celebrity crush hidden.

*(to Nan)* You didn't know about this one either, Nan. It's a good thing, because... you'll see.

My own little secret. Found only beneath the bed sheets, hidden deep within the shiny surface of this ancient artefact:

*He holds up to the light, like a priest giving holy communion, a CD.*

Pulsating pop from another world which would fill me with fear, and shake me up like a bottle of lime-flavoured *Panda Pop* – this was the early 2000s, after all – fizzy, ready to blow, and full of danger in E numbers. This is how I felt every time I tuned into that fifty minutes and eleven seconds long joyride. I was at this album's mercy. And I hadn't even opened the booklet yet...

*He reveals the booklet's interior. It's a photograph of Scissor Sisters, and they look outstanding.*

The textures of the outfits, the swag of the positions, the nonchalance of the faces. Lip-biting, they're calling me to join them. But there's one voice, calling for me louder than any of the others. The central figure in this fivesome. I wonder how it might feel if the feathers from his collar were to rub up against my own. I'm curious to tear even more holes in that fishnet T-shirt of his. He's not of this world, and he says:

*(Singer)* "Nor are you, boy."

Under the covers with my Walkman, listening to the album through the spongy caress of my headphones, he says – to me, and only me:

*(Singer)* "You're disgusting…"

Yes. Yes I am!

*(Singer)* "And you're nasty…"

Correct.

*(Singer)* "And you can grab me!"

> So I do. I grab him, with my right hand –
> sometimes both – and I give into the power
> he has over me. He's going to take me
> somewhere that I can only dream of. He's
> calling me to step from my sepia-toned life
> and into glorious technicolour, just like…
> like…

*"Munchkinland" music again…*

Not now Judy!

*He bursts out of the wardrobe. Gasping for breath. A filthy gym sock in his hand, and he sings an irreverent, chaotic mashup of songs:*

*"Take Your Mama" / "Filthy Gorgeous" / "Any Which Way" by Scissor Sisters*

*The song ends in an explosion of semen-like confetti.*

I never share my crush on Jake Shears with anyone. Not because I'm ashamed, but because... he's mine. Most importantly, I'm his. At the mercy of that sticky, sweaty chest.

*(to Nan)*    I told you it was a good thing that I kept this hidden. Sorry, that all got a bit... blue.

*(to Nan)*    Do you remember any of this? Kylie, Kate Bush? Judy Garland? "Meet Me in St. Louis"? Your old house...? Lipstick?

*He hurries over to the dresser. Trying on another shade of lipstick.*

*(to Nan)*    I'll keep trying 'til I find it!

My nan never leaves the house without her lips painted to perfection. Always the same iconic shade. So I have to get it just right. Because I can't stand up to the Uncle Ignorants of the world without it. Her.

*He steps forward for Nan. Nothing. He wipes off the lipstick, and throws the Jake Shears outfit into the washing machine. The washing machine speaks to him.*

*(to Nan)*    The laundrette! You must remember the laundrette!

A makeshift room at the back of *Waun Fawr*, for over four decades, was the village laundrette, run by Nan. A pile of old magazines on a rickety table. The fabulous women from the village gossiping, as they waited for their washing to finish. All those posters on the big front window:

"Tracy Edwards. Mobile Hairdresser. Competitive prices. Call 07988352636"

Discount for O.A.P.s.

"Caldicot Amateur Operatic Society presents: *Cinderella* – the Panto classic!"

In February...

"LOST CAT: Milo. Recognisable for antisocial behaviour and pink collar." No reward.

It's completely empty now. Just a chipwood shell at the back of the house, slowly being overtaken by nature. Branches growing through the holes in the walls where the massive tumble dryers once sat, and a shutter over the front window. They'll never find Milo now.

*(to Nan)*      Since you haven't lived there for so long now, I guess it doesn't seem right to keep it running... sorry, Nan.

*(to Nan)*      Okay... well, you must remember my teenage years. They weren't so long ago, really. Like when you and I were in *Big Tesco*, Chepstow, doing a food shop, and I pose the idea of a trip to Cardiff for Gay Pride with Meryl.

                Sorry, I should explain: Meryl is a sort of... codename for my best friend.

*(to Nan)*      You'll remember, Dad used to describe him as a brickshithouse in a Hawaiian shirt.

*( Nan)*      "And what do you suppose you'll get up to?"

                I blank. Not because I'm hiding anything, but because I genuinely have... no idea what happens at Gay Pride. Suddenly it doesn't seem like such a good idea.

*(younger self)*  "Never mind. I doubt I'd fit in anyway."

                That signature wicked smile stops me in my tracks.

*(Nan)*      "And since when have you and I cared about fitting in?"

She starts giving me all this advice. "Stick with Meryl at all times. Avoid anyone who looks too under the influence. Don't kiss anyone who appears to be much older than me."

*(younger self)* "Nan!"

*(Nan)*     "I'm not just your nan. I'm your friend too."

I look up – and we're not in the frozen foods aisle anymore, Toto...

*(Nan)*     "I just want to make sure that you're being safe..."

And Nan plops a three-pack of Durex condoms into the trolley. It is accompanied by a mysterious 100ml tube, with a pump. My first bottle of lube. A gift. From my grandmother.

*(to Nan)*     Thank you, Nan...

Pride arrives. Meryl and I cross the threshold into Bute Park with all the confidence of two small-town teen Gayngels. We see boys, holding hands. Drag queens singing shit renditions of *Big Spender*. And lesbians. Real-life lesbians. I clutch my tiny *Robin Ruth* crossbody bag – condoms and lube buried deep within –

close to my hip. I'm terrified. What if Nan's wrong. What if I don't fit in here?

Before I have too long to think about this possibility, we find ourselves in a dingy disco tent. Bass reverberates from tarpaulin walls, flecked with mud, the smell of alcopops permeates the air – along with something rubbery and liquidy. And I'm dancing, trying to have a good time, when I'm pushed up against Jac. With a C, and no K. Kind of greasy dark hair. Tall. Lanky. Handsome. Ish.

We chat, and flirt, I feign shyness, ingenuity, and eventually he leads us out of Bute Park, into the streets of Cardiff and towards a dismal pub, on the corner of Chippy Lane. It looks like somewhere my dad would go for a pint. But as Jac, Meryl and I step inside... I realise, this isn't one of Dad's pubs at all, and I thank our Lady Judy Garland that Dad can't see me now. Because this is *The King's Cross*. This is a gay bar.

*He enters the wardrobe, the fear of a 'baby-gay at his first Grindr hook-up' in his eyes, and steps out in a simple, yellow tulle dress. Sandy Olsson – pre "You're the One That I Want" – eat your heart out. He sings:*

*"Where The Boys Are" by Connie Francis interwoven with the full lowdown of his first Cardiff Pride.*

Jac steps towards me, a touch too close, and my heart stops, forgetting for a second where I am. He kisses me, aggressive, tender, uncomfortable, far too long, but sexy as fuck! I taste his sweaty, sloppy mouth, and pass him the sickly-sweet flavour of *Blue VK* from mine, then we come up for air. He looks right into my aching soul with a tipsy, greasy smile.

I lock eyes with a gurning woman. She's terrifying. Her teeth are chattering, and all I can hear is Nan's voice, telling me to avoid anyone who looks too under the influence, and this woman is definitely under the influence of... something. But it's too late. She's coming over, looks like she's about to take a bite out of my chin, and she says:

*(Woman)* "First Pride, love?"

She knows. She's been where I am before, and she welcomes me into the fold, with a Herculean hug. She gives me a *Sterling Menthol Superking*, which Jac and I twosies. As he whispers into my ear –

*(Jac)*      I'm off for a slash, babe.

*The song ends, and Luke stays in the memory of his first wide-eyed teenage romance for a moment.*

The condoms and lube remained tightly sealed that weekend, and though I never heard from Jac again, I didn't mind. I got everything I needed from my first Pride.

*(to Nan)* Thanks to you Nan, I found somewhere I could go and feel warm, safe, loved. Just like you said I would. A bit like your house, but with cheap booze... and drag queens.

*He takes off the dress and puts it in the washing machine.*

*(to Nan)* Do you remember my first Pride? I need you to remember, Nan. You can't forget any of this, because all the best stuff happens when you're around. And all the worst stuff happens when you're not.

Thirteen-year-old me is having a very private, very important, thirteen-year-old conversation with Allison Moore.

*(Mother)* "What were you talking to Allison about?"
My mother looms large.

*(younger self)* "Nothing."

Too quick to defend. My first mistake.

She obsesses over mine and Allison's conversation for an entire week. Threatens to call Allison and ask her. I call her bluff. My second mistake.

And Allison tells my mother, that I am gay. Over the phone.

Now Mum knows. She darts to the front door, before I even have a chance to talk to her about it. Suddenly, alone in the house, I lock the front door, and it hits me. The realisation that this is my coming out story. Whether I like it or not, it's happening. A knock on the door. My heart races. Banging on the door. I try to ignore it. A booming voice from the other side of the door. It isn't Mum, and it stops my heart dead. But maybe it will be okay. Maybe they'll understand. My third mistake.

Towering over me are two godlike figures. My mother, and devout Christian, Auntie Ann. I face them. Just me. Honest, open, out – me. But it's too late. They don't recognise me. And they don't want this version of me – this version of me that was forced to exist far too soon.

I keep waiting for a third, more powerful god to appear. But she never does.

*Silence. The pianist begins a dark, lonely refrain. And he sings:*

*"Crucify" by Tori Amos / "Jóga" by Björk*


*The song is interrupted by a snap back to a sort of reality.*

> I wake up, in the tiny upstairs bathroom, next to a multipack of cheese and onion crisps. I've camped out here overnight. Alone. And in the absence of my nan, I conjure another ally. A pair of perfect legs, that step out of the shower. It's Kylie Minogue. She looks amazing. She speaks to me:

*(Kylie)* "Chookas, baby."

> Kate Bush is swirling around in the net curtains, she catches my eye, tears one of them down, and places it on my head... like a veil.

*(Kate Bush)* "It's time for your own Tour of Life, darling."

> Soon I'm surrounded by an army of divas. Some that I recognise, some that I'm yet to discover. I grip the hands of two defiant strangers – a flame-haired Cornflake Girl and a Scandinavian nymph. They fill me with a strength that I've never needed before. So I use it.

*He sings one final defiant chorus of the song, which is interrupted once more by a sudden feeling of exposing, bearing his soul, perhaps when he didn't intend to.*

And when I think that my future is just me and my imaginary diva best-friends, against the world, a voice addresses me:

*(Nan)* "Everything okay, sunshine? You can always talk to me. And you know exactly where to find me. Remember. I'm not just your nan. I'm your friend too."

Finally, the more powerful god had appeared. She swept me up in her arms and carried me back to a safe, warm, loving home.

*(to Nan)* Do you remember when I came to live with you in *Waun Fawr*? How you saved me?

*(to Nan)* Okay, do you remember any of this? Your shade of lipstick? Your old house? The Boxing Day parties every year? All the costumes you made me for fancy dress? When I lost my pet hamster in the laundrette? Do you even remember that I'm your grandson, Nan?

*(to Nan)* Because if you don't, what's the point? What am I supposed to do? Am I supposed to forget too?

*(Judy Garland)* "That's showbiz, kid."

Judy Garland is staring back at me in the mirror. Just when I need her, the greatest diva of them all appears.

*(Judy Garland)* "They'll knock us down, but the best fighters, we just get right back up again."

She's a far cry from that wide-eyed ingenue of *Meet Me in St. Louis*. Her eyes look like they've cried enough tears to drown all five of her husbands.

*(Judy Garland)* "So put on a fresh coat of lipstick, go out and do something... for you."

She's right. All this time I've been holding onto Nan. Nan and me. Me and Nan. But at some point, I have to do all of this... just me.

*(to Nan)*     Still, we can have one last adventure together, can't we, Nan? So, what should it be?

*(Judy Garland)* "Why it oughta be a trip to New York to see eight Broadway shows in five days, kid!"

Bang on Judy!

So, we plan the biggest, most exciting adventure of all. While she's still my nan. The nan that doesn't forget things. The nan that isn't living with dementia.

*(to Nan)*     So, will you try to remember when we went to New York together?

*(to Nan)*     Me in a big faux fur coat that we bought from the charity shop in Caldicot. You bartered it down to four pounds because there was a button missing on the sleeve. Me and you walking arm in arm through Times Square... you thought it was daytime because the pavements were so brightly lit by all the billboards. *A Little Night Music.* Starring Bernadette Peters. *Send in the Clowns.* The perfect 11 o'clock number.

*(to Nan)*     It's my most cherished memory of us. You weren't just my nan – you were my friend too. And even as your memories fade, I'll always have it. Even if you won't.

*He looks through the wardrobe one final time, at all of the memories these garments hold. He's looking for the perfect gown for his nan to remember him in. He finds a black and gold, sequined, floor-length dress. He puts it on, ready for his 11 o'clock number:*

*"I Stayed Too Long At The Fair" by Barbra Streisand*

/ *"Send In The Clowns" from "A Little Night Music" by Stephen Sondheim.*

*He reaches into the pocket of his nan's faux fur coat. It's a tube of lipstick. Nan's perfect shade. At last!*

*He takes off the dress, puts it in the washing machine, closes the door, and finally sets it to spin, full of the precious memories of him and his nan.*

It's my nan's ninety-first birthday today. But there's no big party this year. Everyone's got different time slots to visit. Except for me, I stay with her all day. Watching everyone come and go, drop off their gifts, as Nan sits in her chair. Content.

I step outside for some air, and guess who's just arrived? It's Uncle Ignorant. We lock eyes. Something is different between us. It's something he sees in me. Finally, I break the silence.

How are you, darling?

*(to Nan)* And in that moment, I realise I can do this without you, Nan. I can do this without you. And I will. Because you've given me everything I need to survive.

When it's just me and Nan, it's time for my present.

*He puts the lipstick on.*

> Your perfect shade, Nan – *Amethyst Shimmer* by *Rimmel.*
>
> As I help her put it on, those famous eyes of hers – one brown and one blue – light up, and a wicked smile grows through her perfectly-painted lips. She says:

*(Nan)*          "Oh, my sunshine, do you remember when we went to New York together?"

*He fills with pride – the nan that he remembers is still in there. "Optimistic Voices" from "The Wizard of Oz" chimes in merrily, as the Emerald City appears, behind the wardrobe. Finally, a place he can go and survive, on his own. He skips off, into his new life.*

*Lights down.*

*The End.*

# SONGS

### 1. MATERIAL GIRL / DRESS YOU UP***

'Material Girl' (1984) by Peter Brown and Robert Rans 'Dress You Up' (1984) by Andrea LaRusso and Peggy Stanziale, both originally recorded by Madonna, produced by Nile Rodgers, for Sire Records.

2. 'The Trolley Song' (1944) originally recorded by Judy Garland. Produced by MGM Studios for the film *Meet Me in St. Louis*. Music by Hugh Martin, lyrics by Ralph Blane.

### 3. WOW/WOW***

'Wow' (2007) originally recorded by Kylie Minogue, [Incorporating elements of 'Can't Get You Out of My Head' originally recorded by Kylie Minogue, 2001] written by Greg Kurstin, Karen Poole and Kylie Minogue, originally produced by Greg Kurstin and Karen Poole for Parlophone Records Ltd.

'Wow' (1978) written by Kate Bush, originally produced by Andrew Powell for EMI Records.

'Can't Get you Out of my Head' (2001) written by Cathy Dennis and Rob Davis, originally produced by Cathy Dennis and Rob Davis for Parlophone Records Ltd.

### 4. TAKE YOUR MAMA / FILTHY GORGEOUS / ANY WHICH WAY***

'Take Your Mama' (2004) written by J. Shellards and S. Hoffman, originally produced by Neil Harris and Scissor Sisters for Polydor Records.

'Filthy Gorgeous' (2004) written by J. Shellards, A. Lynch and S. Hoffman, originally produced by Neil Harris and Scissor Sisters for Polydor Records.

'Any Which Way' (2010) backing vocals by Kylie Minogue, written by J. Shellards, A. Lynch, S.Hoffman and S. Price, originally produced by Stuart Price and Scissor Sisters for Polydor Records.

5. 'Where The Boys Are' (1960) originally recorded by Connie Francis, produced by Jesse Kaye for MGM Records. Written by Neil Sedaka and Howard Greenfield.

6. CRUCIFY / JÓGA***

'Crucify' (1992) originally recorded and written by Tori Amos, produced by Ian Stanley and Davitt Sigerson for Atlantic Recording Corporation / East West Records

'Jóga' (1997) originally recorded by Björk, written by Björk and Sjón, produced by Björk and Mark Bell for *One Little Indian*.

7. I STAYED TOO LONG AT THE FAIR / SEND IN THE CLOWNS***

'I Stayed too Long at the Fair' (1966) Originally recorded by Barbra Streisand, written by Billy Barnes, produced by Robert Mersey for Columbia Records.

'Send in the Clowns' (1973) written by Stephen Sondheim, originally recorded by Glynis Johns on the Original Broadway Cast Recording of *A Little Night Music* produced by Goddard Lieberson for Columbia Records.

*** *Indicates the listed songs reconceived as a mashup, arranged by Musical Director David George Harrington*

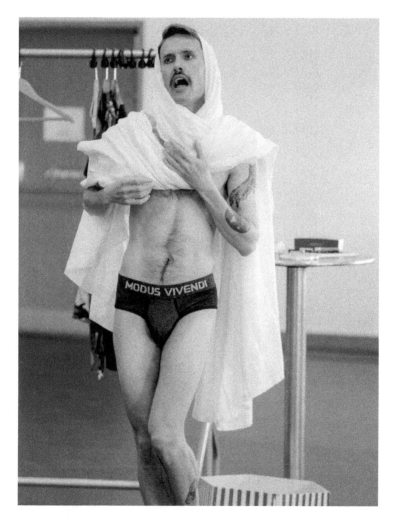

Luke Hereford. Photo: Chris Lloyd

Above and below: Luke Hereford. Photo: Chris Lloyd

Luke Hereford and Joan Hereford, photo: Guto Rhun

**THE CONVERT** by Ben Kavanagh
ISBN 978-1-912430-76-5    £9.99

**NEXT LESSON** by Chris Woodley
ISBN 978-1-912430-19-2    £9.99

**CARE TAKERS** by Billy Cowan
9781910798-81-2    £9.99

**BREATHLESS** by Laura Horton
ISBN 978-1-912430-83-3    £8.99

**NOOR** by Azma Dar
ISBN 978-1-912430-72-7    £8.99

**THE MAKING OF A MONSTER** by Connor Allen
ISBN 978-1-912430-85-7    £8.99

**FREE-FALL** by Ashwin Singh
ISBN 978-1-911501-07-7    £8.99

**THREE WOMEN** by Matilda Velevitch
ISBN 978-1-912430-35-2    £9.99

**PROJECT XXX** by Kim Wiltshire & Paul Hine
ISBN 978-1-906582-55-5    £8.99

**COMBUSTION** by Asif Khan
ISBN 978-1-911501-91-6    £9.99

**DIARY OF A HOUNSLOW GIRL** by Ambreen Razia
ISBN 978-0-9536757-9-1    £8.99

**SPLIT/MIXED** by Ery Nzaramba
ISBN 978-1-911501-97-8    £10.99

**THE TROUBLE WITH ASIAN MEN** by Sudha Bhuchar, Kristine Landon-Smith and Louise Wallinger
ISBN 978-1-906582-41-8    £8.99

More great plays at:
**www.aurorametro.com**

Printed in the USA
CPSIA information can be obtained
at www.ICGtesting.com
JSHW041932030823
45890JS00005B/20